Just Dance With Me

LEON MONTGOMERY

CARITA MONTGOMERY

Contents

Acknowledgments

LEON'S ACKNOWLEDGEMENT

First, I acknowledge Him. I give all praises to my Lord and Savior Jesus Christ who is the head of my life. I raised my children to love the Lord and to listen to Him. Without His guidance I would be lost. I love His teachings on forgiveness. He answers when I call. He healed me when I was filled with a disease. He comforted me when I was lonely. He covered me so times I endured storms in my life. He has been my counselor & lawyer during some really difficult times. He has been my absent mother and father. He has been my friend indeed. I encourage you to get to know him. He is my Everything!!!

I want to acknowledge my children Nia, Kaylan & Joshua Montgomery. You are my very existence because there is an intricate part of me in you all. I know I haven't been the perfect father, but I am so blessed that God allow me to father you. I know there were times you hated & didn't like your daddy. I can assure there are so many good memories which oppose that. That's God's Grace giving me the opportunity to grow as a father. You three are the best guinea pigs a father could have... laughing so hard right now I'm coughing uncomfortably. I thought Carita was my first love.

Nia aka my "Big Baby" you changed that! When you were born, I fell so honestly in love with you. You became my main priority in life. At the same time, I could be the strongest man in the world, but the weakest with you. I couldn't say no to you. All I wanted to do was spoil you & give whatever you wanted. You & I have had some unique battles. No matter how much you fought and hated (at times) me, I never left or let you down. I'm blessed with you, and that is something I have never taken for granted. You look like your mother, but you have the behavior of me, attitude, temperament & quick tongue. Thank you for strengthening me as a father.

Kaylan aka my "Lil Bit" you have a unique beginning. My second born and you are that middle child like me. When you were still in the womb, I felt a closer connection with you more than ever. It was like you can hear my voice when I would come around. When your mom and I was in bed at night, you would go on a kicking spree. While cuddling with your mom, you would be kicking so hard, I would get up and be like what in the hell is going on with him? Yes, I thought sure you was going to be a boy because I didn't think girls could kick so hard. Little did I know. I cried when you were born. I thought you was going to be a boy. I know I laugh about it now... lol Like your sister, once I looked into them big eyes, I fell in love all over again. Growing up, you was a child who didn't give me any trouble. When you became older so did your voice. The shy & reserved young lady spoke up & loudly. You live a life of introvert, but that is not you. You were the first child to tell her father how it was going to be and that I was going to listen to you. It was hard to fight or discipline you because I NEVER HAD TO. I know you look more like me and act so freaking much like your mom. Thank you for teaching me patience & understanding,

Joshua aka my "Prince of South aka my "Big Fella". You are a dream come true! I prayed for you! You are a mix of your mom and me. You didn't look or act like me. I was worried if he was going to be able to hang with these girls. They claim you broke a lot of things around the house. I wasn't hearing a four-year-old was capable of such. I figured they blamed you because you were the youngest. Little did I know! It was you breaking and destroying things in the house. He is four years old & the girls said he broke the handle on the clothes hamper. I was like nawh, he ain't strong enough to do that. I forgot, during your birth you was flexing muscles with wide-open eyes. As an older child you are still flexing your muscles at sixteen years old. Joshua, you possess a certain positive spirit about you. Due to all the police killings & brutality on black and brown skins, I am overprotective with you. I'm just scared to lose you. I don't want to lose my teenage son to the police or to street violence. Thank you for helping me be a better Health Professional, Mentor, Coach, Spiritual Guidance, Father and more importantly a Friend. I love our conversations.

The ultimate acknowledgement goes to my parents Leon & Mary Montgomery for giving me life. I'm blessed! Roxie Ann Davis is my MVP acknowledgment. She sacrificed and gave up so much to raise me and my siblings. My primary goal was to take care of you, mama. But I know you wouldn't want the focus on you. It was you who taught me how to love a woman & to be a man. There's a saying a woman can't teach a boy how to be a man! I totally disagree. Most of what I learned came from my grandmother, RAD. She is my HERO! Thanks mama for sacrificing.

My siblings James Tatum (Deceased), Jeffrey Davis & Melissa Montgomery. I thank you for being who you are. Being my siblings made me who I am. I know I am not the perfect brother, but I thank you for allowing me to be who I am. I love and respect you for who you are. No matter how much we argue & fight, we are going to remain siblings. One Love.

The entire extended Lazier family. My grandmother Curleane Lazier was the only person who saw something more in me. I'm not blood, but I sure wish I was. It was her who listened to me when I was hurt & didn't know it. She walked with me to the altar at St. Stephens Church and I gave my life to Christ. I am so grateful! I truly love mama Lazier, aunts, uncles & endless cousins.

I've always acknowledged my blood uncles & aunts Buster, Pee Wee, Aunt Ella, Richard, Ricky, Roe & Jo Davis. Thank you all! You're a part of me forever.

Special Acknowledgements to my Godfather, Mentor & frat brother Pastor James E. A Stephens. He volunteered to take care and mentor me. He is still that father figure in my life.

He made sure I went off to college with money. I had no scholarship offers. He took care of me like I was his own. I loved the fact that his son and I both attended HBCUs in the Atlanta University Center (AUC). He helped me get my driver's license. Thanks pops!

Jo Ann and Raymond Henderson have been in my life forever! Her parents have been prominent in my grandparent's life. She has been so instrumental in my young life. She drove me to work each week at Southeast Bank. She has been in all my & children's life. She is my family. She has blessed me so much; she is so amazing.

CARITA'S ACKNOWLEDGEMENT

I would like to acknowledge God who is the head of my life. I can do all things through Christ that strengthens me.

I want to acknowledge my husband Leon who is always so supportive of all my dreams and crazy ventures. Thank you for never killing my dreams. You are truly the wind beneath my wings.

To my beautiful kids Nia, Kaylan and Joshua, I have always taught you that the sky is the limit. Follow your dreams and never give up. God is with you always.

I want to acknowledge my mother who raised my siblings and me to have a love for reading and learning. It is because of her that I am inspired to be an author today. I love you, Jean. To my father Ben (Henry) for being my support system throughout college.

To my twin sister Carisa, I love you for being my best friend. To my big sister Davilyn, I love you for always helping me dream big dreams, and to my older brother Ricky thank you for being my mentor.

Thanks to everyone who made this project come to life Sherilyn for Designing the amazing cover, to Takara for your editing and Kimberly for final publishing.

CHAPTER 1

When We First Met

LEON'S POINT OF VIEW

> *Proverbs 18:22 Whoso findeth a wife findeth a good thing, and obtaineth favour of the Lord.*

I met Carita when I was in Church. I was singing with my youth gospel choir, the Agape, and I was in the choir with my cousins and some friends, and we noticed two new faces in the front Pew. My cousin Keith and I said, hey, we're going to go down and talk to these girls after Church. Lo-and-behold, we did. We discovered they were twins. We saw the twins outside in their car after service. We approached the car and asked for their names and got their numbers. I liked the other twin. But of course, she didn't like me. She liked another friend of mine.

But either way, we end up getting their phone numbers. And we talked back and forth throughout that summer. I think the following summer, I was on this youth program. I forget the name, but I was working with a youth group for the summer job, I was in a van and we were actually working on the beach, and I knew where the twins lived because they actually lived next door to my cousins. As we were leaving the beach this day, I was driving. I had my driver's license, so the supervisor; he was this older guy he allowed me to drive. I said, hey, do you mind if I swing by my girlfriend's house? Well, she wasn't my girlfriend at the time. But he said, wow, you have a girlfriend that lives in Sarasota? I said, yeah. So, he allowed me to drive by.

I went and knocked on the door and keep in mind, I was in a 15-passenger van with probably 10 to 12 people in youth boys in the van. Carita came out, and we started talking. She was shocked to see me at her door. So, I think I asked her, can we go out to a movie or something? And she agreed. And I think I stopped to talk about five minutes, and from there we talked almost every day.

I pursued her. I visited her often. We went out on dates, dinner dates, like I said, going to the movies, and we just hung out a lot. That's how I end up meeting Carita for the first time when I started visiting her home. I didn't think her mom liked me as much, probably because I visited her home way too much. And I think she didn't like that. But I continue to come over and visit. And also, Rita came over and visit, and sometimes a few times she missed her curfew, and I'm pretty sure that would make her mom upset and a little hesitant about her seeing or dating me because one I lived in Bradenton which is several miles from Sarasota. But I can understand her reasoning for not wanting her to date me now. I was not a bad boy at that time. I mean, I've had my share of fights and suspensions while in middle school, but never in high school.

I think I was a good model student. I pretty much had

my act together. By the time I got into high school, and I was beginning to be popular, I played football and ran track. I also was active in social clubs. I also created my own club in high school called "S.T.O.P." (Students today opposing Prejudice). I received the NAACP Award for an article I wrote regarding an incident that took place at our bus stop, where a group of white boys on the back of a truck threw a hand grenade. It sparked a lot of racial tension in our community, especially at my school.

I thought Carita was a beautiful, intelligent young lady, and I was destined to have her in my life. I was going to make every attempt to keep her in my life. I think she was good for me. She was motivated, she was caring. I mean, it's amazing how much she has done for others at a very young age. I saw her take care of her nephews daily. I saw her maybe once or twice over the weekend and just the things that she's done for them. Same thing with her grandmother.

I know she takes her grandmother shopping every Saturday morning like clockwork with no one telling her to do it or anyone asking her to do it. She loved her mom, grandmother, and her aunt. She was very close to them, and she made it clear to me in the beginning, when we first started dating that they were her priority. Don't plan things and activities or visit her during those hours because taking care of her family was a top priority, and I respected it that made me happy, you know, that she was caring like that.

And there's one thing that I loved about her, well liked about her. Love came down a little further down the road, but love eventually came again. Rita, she had it all together straight-A student, performing arts student who wouldn't want a person like that in their life. Honestly, I think she just made me better, and that was attractive, but it just made me want more in life as well.

So, I knew she was going to eventually going off to school. So, I still had to make plans for myself and what my plans are going to be after high school. So, I became motivated and decided, hey, I'm going to go off to College as well, but I also was contemplating about entering the Army. I took ASVAB, I was going down to sign my papers to go into the Army but got cold feet and thought about war and being away for so long that I didn't want to risk the chance of losing Carita or losing anybody in my family for being away for so long. So, I decided not to go into the Army and decided to attend college. And I ended up enrolling at Morris Brown College in Atlanta, Georgia.

When I first met Carita, she had a very close, tight knit family. She was being raised by a single mom. I knew nothing about her father, but I learned to love and appreciate her grandparents. I got to meet some of her uncles, her brother, her sisters. Very close family. Another thing that I loved about being around them. I didn't get to see much of that closeness in my own family. And if anybody who knows me, I'm a family-oriented guy, so I enjoy hanging around them and spending holidays and enjoying some of their cultural activities.

When I met Carita, I brought her around my grandmother as well as my family, which my grandmother adored Carita. She thought she was the best thing since sliced bread for me. So, I have brought some other girls home to meet my grandmother that she didn't approve of. So, when I brought Carita to meet her for the first time, she thought she was just a breath of fresh air. She had everything she liked, how she was smart, articulate, intelligent, and she was ambitious. My grandmother loved it. And I wish Carita could have spent more time with her as well before she passed on. But my grandmother was very fond of her. So, we would eat dinner and stuff like that. And I also took her around my spiritual family. I'm very fond of them. They are my extended family. They are true and dear to my heart. We would attend Church and come home to grandmother house for Sunday dinner with the entire family. And I would bring Carita. And we're used to sitting outside for Sunday dinner, playing cards, talking trash and doing whatever. And I enjoy sitting outside eating.

Carita is not the type that likes to eat outside. The flies and the gnats and all these insects are aggravating to her. She didn't want to eat with them around her food. Every other minute she felt like she was getting bitten by a mosquito and it just hurt me that she just can't sit outside and have a good time. So that was a good fun memory of us first meeting and dating, sitting outside trying to eat and she just couldn't do it with the insects and the flies and so forth. So that is something that I felt like I needed to share in this book. She can be paranoid sometimes.

But things changed over time. Meeting her was, I don't know, different, very different. And I will just leave it at that for right now. As we were dating, I asked Carita, did she have a boyfriend? And she said she did not have one. But, it was some guy who was interested in her and I don't know, maybe they spoke once or twice. I forget his name, but I was going to make it my business that this dude did not have a chance in hell getting her. So, I made my presence known. So, I guess that end of how we first met.

CARITA'S POINT OF VIEW

> *Proverbs 31: 10 -11 Who can find a virtuous woman? for her price is far above rubies.[11] The heart of her husband doth safely trust in her, so that he shall have no need of spoil.*

When we first met. Well, we got to go way, way, way, way back. We met in Church. Surprisingly, Leon was in the choir that night, I think, and me and my twin sister were in the audience. My mom and her choir sung that night. It was like a choir reunion or some type of night Church service. But anyway, I saw him. He saw me. But I think he didn't even like me.

At first. I think he liked my sister but that's a long story. I don't know how me and him ended up hooking up. I think somehow, they got our phone numbers. We got their phone numbers. It was a group of them. But fast forward, I think it was my junior year and I had a dream. Believe it or not, about a guy named Leon. And I had totally forgotten about the Leon I met at Church that night. But my junior year, he came to my house with a van full of kids on a youth program. Knocked on my door. I didn't know he knew I existed. Didn't know he knew where I lived. But he showed up. And I think that's where the romance kind of started.

When Leon and I first met, I really hadn't dated. I liked this boy. I had a little relationship type thing where I had a crush on this guy. He walked me home from school a couple of times, gave me some Valentine's Day candy and Carnation and stuff like that, but just hadn't really had a romance. So, when Leon came along, I don't know. Something sparked. He had a bit of this bad boy edge on him. He was a romantic. He liked to write poems. He played football. He was popular. I don't know. All of this was a recipe, I guess, for romance, I think. On the other hand, I was the good girl. We grew up in Church. We weren't allowed to just hang out. We stayed close to home, a close knit family, very involved with our grandparents and uncles and cousins. Just kind of a good girl. Good grades in school. Never got in trouble in school. Never. Not during high school. I didn't get in trouble. I just wasn't that type of girl. But you get where I'm going with this good girl bad guy kind of thing.

That was our junior year. Then there was senior year. We had become serious girlfriend and boyfriend. Everybody knew we were a couple. And so, we dated throughout our senior year. And we did homecoming and prom and grad night and all the things that high school seniors do together. We had the matching clothes, the pictures at Sears, we went to the movies. We hung out at the beach like a great romance, like a Romeo and Juliet type thing, because I came from a home in the suburbs. And Leon grew up in the housing projects. So, you can understand a bit of the push and pull there as well. But it was love.

We were in love. We were inseparable. We talked on the phone for hours and hours and hours. It was fun. It was something that I enjoyed doing and no strings attached. It's what we wanted to do. And after graduation, I knew I was going off to college. That was always the plan. Of course, the good girl who makes the good grades is going to go off to college. Of course she is. So I got accepted into FAMU,

Florida A&M University, and I went off to school. I was on my own for the first time. I had this boyfriend who went off to a different school. He went off to Morris Brown College in Atlanta, Georgia, and we just had to figure life out from that point.

CHAPTER 2

Our first Argument

LEON'S POINT OF VIEW

> Be ye angry, and sin not: let not the sun go down upon your wrath Eph 4:26

Well, for me, she really, really didn't argue. The argument really started with me. I was just angry a lot, and for no reason. I didn't know why I was angry. I know our earliest arguments probably started when I felt she was spending too much time with her family and not enough time with me and my side of the family. And she made it clear in the beginning before we even started dating that taking care of her grandmother was her number one priority, her grandmother, her great aunt and her mom, if need be the nephews. And in the beginning, it was all well, but as time went by, it just seemed like she was spending more and more time with them, and it was becoming less and spending less time with me and that did make me angry. And I really don't know why I was so angry about that. That's the thing that I loved about her, that she cared for others. She'll put others before herself.

And she has always been that way. That's one of the characteristics that I love and adore.

We didn't do much on my mom's side of the family. We didn't do holidays with other families. We didn't do family reunions; we didn't do a lot of family activities. We celebrated Christmas and Thanksgiving, but we just didn't have the family tight-knit group of people coming over the house and enjoying a meal and fellowship. We didn't have that. However, on my dad's side of the family, the Montgomery, we did that and a lot more. We spent holidays together and Thanksgiving and we talked, and we were there for each other. And I appreciate my cousins. I feel that is what made me angry a lot because I didn't get to have that tight knit family like Carita did with her family.

We argued about that, and we fought and again, it really wasn't her. It was all me. Over the years, you know, going off to College and I've gone my way. She's gone hers and we don't see and talk to each other as much. That also made me angry. I would call her dorm, and she's not there, or she was not available. She was playing card games, or she was hanging out with her friends. I wasn't really hanging out doing those types of things. And when I called upon her, she wasn't there. So that made me angry. And we would fight over the phone. I was not living in the dorm. I was living with my Uncle, and he, oh, man, he was like another father to me. He was my everything. He understood me more than anybody. But to make a long story short, when we did talk, we ran up his phone bill. I still didn't talk to her as much as I wanted to, but it is what it is. And she was living her life with her friends and new friends, and she's doing what she needed to do. I should have been taking advantage of doing what I needed to be doing.

I remember this one time we started arguing, and I became not only verbally abusive, but I became physical as well. She was living in Phenix City, Alabama, and our argument became physical, and I ended up striking her and hitting her in the mouth and splitting her lip. I don't know why or what caused me to do that. I can't even remember what we even fought about, but I ended up cutting her lip and she had to have stitches, and I ended up getting arrested as well. So that is the first altercation that I can recall that we ever had. And over the years, that became more and more. I am not proud of this at all. And I take full responsibility because again, I was just angry and don't know why I was angry. I had other relationships where I was also physically abusive. I grew up in a home where my grandparents were physically abusive. And that's all I saw. Fighting and cussing at one another striking one another. I don't know. That's what I saw. I thought that was normal.

I should not put my hands on another person, another female, and it wasn't normal. It was just the environment I grew up in, which was abnormal. And it took me years to realize that what I was doing was wrong, and it was hurting people, especially the ones that I care for. So that was just the first. There were many more. I remember there was a time that she called the police for every little thing I did. If I was cursing too loud or I cursed in front of the children. I think we had kids, but I went too far. She called the police. I mean, she had 911 on speed dial, and they were just constantly coming to the house for every little thing, or, you know, most of the time I leave before the police even get there. These arguments and fights over the years did result in us splitting up, not seeing each other anymore, giving each other some time to think about what's best for each other. Allow me probably to get the help that I needed and which I did. I ended up going to counseling, individual counseling alone. then eventually I asked Carita if she would join me in counseling so we can be on one page if we decide to continue our relationship. She agreed. And we did do the counseling.

I felt like the counseling did help, and we just took it one day at a time and continued to live our lives, not saying that there were no other fights or arguments, which there were, but sometimes just got to know how to deal with them and sometimes you need to walk away and give each other some time and space and then come back together and see if we're able to sit down and communicate. In hindsight, it was kind of comical because we didn't know how to argue. I would get upset with Carita and she would start yelling. She's good at yelling and raising her voice, and that triggers me to use foul language and profanity and so forth, and I would ask her not to do that. She felt like she couldn't get her point across if she was not yelling it and I wasn't going to allow her to yell at me without throwing some stones at her. I know her triggers.

She doesn't like to be called out her name, and she don't like me using profanity, but her yelling was my trigger. We just didn't know how to properly communicate, and I think that's where a lot of our issues came from. If I disagreed, she disagreed, then okay, here we go. It's going to start an argument, and we just didn't know how to argue, agree to disagree. And it's just made things worse in our relationship. It really did. I often ask myself, why did she stay? Because she didn't have to put up with the abuse, any type of abuse, physical or verbally. But I often ask myself, why did she stay? Everything I was doing was not normal.

CARITA'S POINT OF VIEW

Let me start with communication from my standpoint. You see, I never saw communication between a husband and a wife. I grew up in a single parent home with just my mother. There was never a chance for me to see a husband and wife interact. To see a mother and father have agreements, have disagreements, have conflict, and for me to see how that conflict could be positively resolved. So, I grew up with a jaded perception. It was just my mom. There were no arguments in my house. Sometimes she had to discipline us, the children, but there were no arguments. So, I thought that a home was supposed to have no conflict. I was jaded, so I didn't have a place to draw from. I didn't have reference points in my own mind how to resolve a conflict with my mate, with my boyfriend, with my spouse. I had nothing to draw from.

Any time an argument arose, and most times it would be Leon getting angry with me and I would lose it because I'm like, this is not the way the world is supposed to work. This is not how I grew up. I don't understand arguing. I don't understand conflict. I don't understand a male figure in the home being angry. I never saw that growing up, and especially once we had our own kids. To me, the arguments were like breaking points, like lines in the sand. I didn't want my kids to experience arguing in the home because I never experienced it. For me, I escalated it because I wanted it to end, like stop arguing, stop yelling. And in the interim, I think I know I would raise my voice because I didn't know how to end it. I wasn't a person to fight. I wasn't a fighter, so I would just escalate my voice to say, hey, enough. I want this arguing to end. I want it to stop.

I love being in a relationship. I love being married. I'm a person who is a thinker. I go back and think a lot about what was said, how it transpired. Sometimes you can say that I might even be an overthinker, but I go back and I replay every single word of an argument. I'll replay it over and over and over and over in my mind to the point that it makes me ill; Almost. I'm saying all of this to say that there were arguments. I didn't have the proper communication tools.

I didn't know how to resolve them properly, and let's just say things probably got out of hand for me, the very first argument that was significantly out of control, and I blame myself for it just as much as I blame my husband. But it was early in the relationship, and I can't remember if we were still in high school or it was our freshman year in college, but we were home. We were at Leon's house, and I don't even know what we were arguing about, but we were both so upset in that the argument.

I went to go get into my car, and he followed me out to my car. Then the argument was outside in his front yard. I just remember, people could see us. People could hear us. I felt hot, flush in my face because I was so embarrassed. I don't want people to see me in an argument. I'm a very private person, and I remember just asking him, begging him, lower your voice, lower your voice. People can hear and that made him escalate even more because he was like, I don't care. I don't care who can hear. But for me, it was such an embarrassing place to be.

I don't want to argue in front of other people. Then I remember his brother came outside and his brother began to try to referee the argument. I'm like, what is this? Why can't we control our tempers? Why can't we control what is being said? Why is there someone else intervening? What is this? I felt like everything was spinning out of control. And then when I looked at him, Leon had such a rage in his eyes. And I think he talks about this in his portion, that he was just angry, and he was just angry. He didn't know why he was so angry. But I saw rage, and I didn't like it. I didn't like what I saw, and it was a bit intimidating. When I saw the rage, and it was probably for me, a red flag. It was a red flag!!

It is a red flag. But once again, not having a reference point how to resolve conflict and how to communicate in that type of situation, that type of environment. I didn't know what to do. I wanted to get in the car and leave. I was attempting to get in the car and leave, but he didn't want me to leave. He wanted to continue the argument. He grabbed the keys. Now, at that point, I felt like you violated all my space, all of my private space. That's my possession. Those are my keys. That's my car. I felt completely violated. But once again, why had it escalated to that point? Why was this happening? Why was there not any resolve earlier on so that it didn't have to reach this point?

This is where I am praying for those that read this chapter that we talk to our young couples. Women talk to the young women. Men talk to the young men. Help them to understand that it's okay to agree to disagree, but it's never okay for an argument to escalate to where it becomes physical. Talk to our young men and women. Let's give them conflict resolution early in their relationships. This book is about healing. This book is about preserving marriages and preserving them in the right way. This book is about each party feeling valued, each party feeling that they are worthy to have an opinion, to get their point across, to disagree, but never to the point of physical altercation.

Now, I couldn't leave. It was minutes, maybe an hour later, I couldn't leave, and I did not like that feeling. It's so destructive. It takes away everything from your being. It is not a good place to be. And as we moved on in our marriage, it continued to be an issue. But there is a place that you can move past, and we're going to share that in other chapters.

CHAPTER 3

Starting a Family

LEON'S POINT OF VIEW

> Behold, what manner of love the Father hath bestowed upon us, that we should be called the sons of God 1John 3:1

Behold, what manner of love the Father hath bestowed upon us, that we should be called the sons of God 1John 3:1

We never talked about starting a family when we were dating. But as we got older and went off to school, we did end up having a daughter in our senior year of college. This was the happiest day of my life. I love that little girl there to death. Love that little girl to the moon and back. I gave her everything she could ever imagine. I feel like my life was on a good path.

Then we got married. My oldest daughter was five years old when we got married. This was the time Carita and I just started to discuss having children. I had a daughter now I wanted a son. My wife was gun ho about having twins. She being a twin and my father and his sister are twins. She felt like we should have twins now. I just wanted a son, and I would have felt our family was complete. But it didn't happen that way.

2 years until she got pregnant again, and we had another daughter, Kaylan Mary, my oldest, is Nia. When Kaylan was born, I kind of cried. When she was in the womb, I used to read to her, rub my wife's belly, kiss her belly. I would talk to the baby, and she would always hear me, and she understood everything I was saying. She was just kicking, and that was confirmation that she heard every word I said. I thought, oh my God, I said, that's going to be a little boy. I said, yeah, I know the way he was kicking. I said, I got myself a little field gold kicker. So, all this time I said, yeah, this is a little boy. I wasn't worried about that is a boy. We did the ultrasound and found out that my second born was also a girl. She was a girl, and I cried because I was disappointed. I thought, Shoot, I had a boy.

She was born, and I held her for the first time. I fell in love all over again. She was my little Leon. Her first three or four years. She was with her dad every day. I worked at a child development center where she attended school. She was with her dad everywhere I went, she went, I go to the Barber shop, she was at the Barber shop. I would drive by to see my brother or friends. She was there, and they always would say she looked like her dad. She acted like her mother. But she was my joy too. My girls were my heart. And I would do anything for those girls. Anything! I wouldn't let anyone hurt them or disrespect them, they were my joy.

There was a time and I have never discussed this with anybody other than my wife, and only a few people know of this, but my wife got pregnant before we had our first child and her family pressured her to have an abortion. Of course, we were young, and she had a future to think about. I want to respect what her family was trying to do. But, I was young too, and I didn't have a job. We did complete high school, and we were freshmen in college, but either way, we were just too young to have a child. So, I was disappointed. I've always thought back in hindsight, that would have been my first son. I think my wife now feels the same. We probably would have had a boy that first time around, but not sure how my wife is going to feel about this story being placed in the book, but we decide to be transparent as possible. So, there it is. I never spoke of this to anyone in my family. Starting the family was far, far from our minds at that time, but it's just something that happened that shouldn't happen at a young age.

As the years went by, we kept saying we were going to keep trying until we have a son. I really wasn't trying. But my wife was into fitness back then. She was working out with a trainer twice a day. She was working out for several months. She had lost a lot of weight. She was physically fit and healthy. It just happened. Her trainer had told her. You're looking good, nice and tone. You're going to end up getting pregnant. And my wife just laughed and brushed it off like, Nah, that ain't going to happen. She didn't tell me this. I heard this after the fact. So sure enough, she got pregnant again, and we didn't want to know the sex of the child but ended up giving in and finding out.

This time I didn't get my hopes up high. Continue kiss and rub and love on my wife's stomach and just pray that I have a son. Lo-and-behold, in 2005 we had a son another one of the happiest day of my life, no matter what he can carry on my name. I was going to name him Leon Montgomery III. My daughter Kaylan who was 4 years old predicted months ago that we are going to have a boy. So somehow, she started calling him Joshua. I mean, for months she would say Joshua. She read to Joshua. I'm going to get Joshua this and that. I'm going to take care of Joshua. Blah, blah, blah, everything, Joshua, Joshua. She said it so much that it stuck with us all. We all started calling him Joshua, though we didn't know that for sure it was a boy. And she didn't even have a backup name just in case it was a girl. No, Jessica, or nothing. She just said Joshua and that she knew and was confident that it was a boy. He was born, and I felt compelled to name him Joshua anyhow. He has my full name, but he has Joshua in front of Leon.

I have an older cousin who would tease me. Oh my God, she would tease me endlessly about not being able to make a boy. Her son made boys. His oldest child is a girl. But afterwards he would make nothing but boys, three of them, to be exact. She would just tease me. You don't know how to make no boys. You need to do this, and you need to do that, and then the method struck a chord with me. She would also say, hey, you do realize you are the last Montgomery, so if you don't have a son, you won't have anybody to carry on your last name. She was right. So, I felt like I was under a lot of pressure. Being naïve, I did the things that she said I should do. I'm not going to say what they were, but I did them. I can't confirm her method 100%. I don't know who else she has told to do those things, but I may have to do a poll on this someday and get results, but let's just say it worked in my favor. We had a boy. Yeah, he was born smiling, and he was born flexing his muscles. He was my joy, too. I was happy that I'll be able to carry on to the Montgomery name through my son.

We have three kids, and they are pretty spread apart. I think the girls are like six years apart. Josh is 5 years apart from the youngest girl. So, we felt like he was going to grow up alone. I've always discussed with my wife about adopting some younger child so he wouldn't be alone growing up. The girls do girl things, and they got each other and things in common opposed to him being the youngest child and a male, and they may not have much in common. So, we talked about it, just talked about it, but never made a decision to adopt. In a way, I regret it. Maybe we could have made a major decision to do it and change some child's life forever for the best.

Although I thank God for allowing me to start my own family with Carita. We tried to raise them the best we could. My wife was raised a certain way, and I was raised a certain way, so I was the disciplinary, and it was hard trying to discipline them when you love them so much and you do it out of love, not out of anger, disappointment, anything like that.

CARITA'S POINT OF VIEW

Starting a Family Well, just like some 21-year-old College students who are kind of just figuring things out on your own, I found myself in a position where I was pregnant. I was in college. I was kind of confused. I wanted to pursue getting my degree, a career. I wanted to be this high-powered corporate executive, and a child just was not on the radar. But here I was finishing up my junior year of college and found myself pregnant. Leon and I wanted to keep this child. I had a previous abortion that I am not happy about, but it just was where I was in my life. So, I was excited about this child that we were about to birth.

I was excited about Leon and I doing it together. I knew it would be challenging, but I saw God in it. I saw a vision before our oldest daughter was ever born. And God came to me in my apartment. Leon and I were in separate cities. I was in Tallahassee, Florida attending FAMU, and he was in Atlanta, Georgia. I was in my apartment alone. And I was looking through the door to the bathroom. And on the wall of the bathroom, Jesus' face came to me clear as day. And he was speaking to me, kind of assuring me that everything was going to be okay.

Our daughter was born. She was the most beautiful baby you could ever want to see. Of course, every parent says that. And from that point on, I knew I had to go hard. My family wanted me to leave school after having the baby was born to come home so I could have help financially and physically. Leon was in college. He was in Atlanta at Morris Brown College. I didn't want to come home. I didn't want to end my college career. There was something in me that said, you can do both. You can be an amazing mother and you can finish your college degree and finish with honors. I walked across the stage and received my college diploma, Bachelor of Science in Business. I was excited about that. The child brought Leon and I closer.

We started dreaming about being a family. We weren't married yet. Five years later we were married. But I think we always knew that we would be together as a family. We talked about how we would raise the child. To be honest, spiritual, successful and all the above. Our first child was probably very spoiled. We went over and above.

We did too much, and we had to learn how to pull that

back later as we had child number two, our second daughter and child number three, our son. We made a lot of mistakes. I grew up in a single parent home. He grew up in a single parent home we didn't have the example of co-parenting together in the same house. We didn't have the example of how we would discipline our children how we would reward our children, what we would do to invest in their futures we just had single parent perspectives and not cohesive co-parenting perspective. We made a lot of mistakes and we had to pray through some of them. Some of them caused us an extreme amount of tension fights, arguments even one caused us separation but none the same we were excited about starting a family about being a family about having this thing that we call a family unit.

I wish we read a parenting manual. I wish we had been given parenting instructions. I wish there were someone to step in and show us how to do this thing correctly, but we had to kind of figure it out on our own and the bumps, the bruises, the mistakes we had to just go through life and figure it out. I'm glad we stuck it out I'm glad we decided we would stay married, and we figure out how to raise these children and here we are today 24 years together started a family, raised a family and we're back to being and loving us again.

CHAPTER 4

Church

LEON'S POINT OF VIEW

> *For a day in thy courts is better than a thousand. I had rather be a doorkeeper in the house of my God, than to dwell in the tents of wickedness. Psalm 84:10.*

I remember the day my grandmother and I joined St. Stephens AME church. That is when I became even closer to my extended family in that Church. I grew up in the Church, done a lot, learned a lot, served God learned about God and the Bible. I served, sang in the youth choir, enjoyed growing up in the Church. Fortunately, my wife and I both grew up in the AME Church. She attended Greater Hurst Chapel AME Church, and we would go to YPD meetings and conferences and fellowship. Not only did I meet her in the Church, but I've also seen her around in community gatherings.

I always thought that we would be in the Church, even dating. We attended Church together. When I went off to College, I also found AME churches to attend. I attended AME Church when I moved to Atlanta, the oldest AME

Church in Georgia. So, when we got married, it was only right that we continue the tradition and attend an AME Church, and we did.

We attended Big Bethel AME. Our girls were active in the Church, and we met some great people within the Church. Pastor was awesome. We just grew and learned. But it was a point where my wife just wanted more. After this pastor has left the Church, she felt like she also wasn't being spiritually fed. Me, I was happy. I was ushering at the time at time, my daughter was attending Sunday school, but my wife just felt like she wasn't growing. She wanted to attend another Church and end up discovering this Megachurch. I didn't want any part of no Megachurch. I felt like our Church was big enough. She would take the girls and they would go visit this Megachurch. I kept going to Big Bethel, and that's where the split and the divide came.

Carita is strong willed and head strong. She can be a little stubborn at times. I know I am, and I was like, no, I don't want nothing to do with a Megachurch. If you are going, then go! She did. And she kept going. She kept going, and she was loving the pastor and loving his teaching. Carita was excited with his preaching and Bible teachings. So eventually they joined the. I was attending the AME Church, and that just didn't sit well with me. At first it did. I was like, I don't care. Do what you want to do. And over time I felt like, no something is not right.

I don't think this is how it should be. I know God wasn't pleased with us worshipping separately. But at the same time, we were giving praise to him. I know He would want us to worship as a family. So, all the while my wife was begging me to come just visit. See if you like it. You can't say you don't like something if you never tried it. But I wouldn't hear of it. She kept poking and poking at me and asking and asking repeatedly. So, I decided to visit. I went and to my surprise, I enjoyed my worship experience there.

This Church is massive, and it was a little overwhelming. The traffic is horrific. The Church is so big, and they have Sheriff's directing traffic on every side of the Church. I visited a couple of times and eventually I liked it. What I liked the most was the Bible teaching. I probably hadn't learned so much from the Bible in all my years as I did in the little, short time I was attending that Megachurch. I learned a lot and picked up my Bible on my own and started reading it. I felt fulfilled. I was being led and eventually I liked it. I think my wife probably was already a member of that Church like 4 years before I joined that Mega-church, and I eventually joined the Church.

CARITA'S POINT OF VIEW

I grew up in the Church. Church was a part of our everyday life. You see, for me, Church was not optional. Church was how do I say this… It was not demanded, it was expected. We were expected to be in Church every Sunday. We were expected to be in a choir rehearsal. We were expected to do church and youth activities. We were expected to be in Sunday School, Sunday Morning Service and Sundy Evening Service. Church was everything. And I wanted Church to be a big part of our family as well. I had a very different dynamic watching Church as a child. My grandmother attended an African Methodist Episcopal Church and my mother and all my uncles and my cousins and my siblings. we all attended that Church with her.

. . .

My grandfather attended a different Church. He attended a local Baptist Church. I never understood why they did not worship together. That experience may be why I did what I did midway our marriage. But let's start here. When we married we both understood that Church was going to be a big part of our family dynamic. My husband was very familiar with Atlanta, so we kind of went wherever he decided we would worship. We originally started out going to a Church in downtown Atlanta. The name escapes me now, but then we finally migrated over to Big Bethel African Methodist Episcopal Church, and we started worshipping there.

We enjoyed it. We met other married couples that had children that were the same age as our oldest daughter. And then when our second daughter was born, we continued worshipping there. And it was familiar, and it was routine. It was a part of our regular behavior that on Sundays we would get up and my husband and I both agreed on the 08:00am Service since we are early birds. We were out of there by 10:00am. I would head to the grocery store and get Sunday dinner. I would prepare dinner. We would eat dinner and watch movies. I would do the children's hair, prepare them for the week. And this was our regular routine. Every Sunday. Every week, month in, month out, year in, year out. But then sometime around 2004/2005. We were married in 1998 so around the 7-year mark. Somewhere around that time, I felt I was not being fed by the Church we were attending. And I was seeking more. I needed more. I needed to grow. I needed to have a pastor that I could relate to.

I needed experiences that were different from what the African Methodist Church was providing me. I grew up in that denomination. I spent 30 years in that denomination. I started branching out, attended and visited some different churches, some different vibes, some different experiences. Then I landed on World Changes Church International. It was five minutes from our house. We were traveling 20-25 minutes to downtown Atlanta to Church and World Changers Church International was literally five to six minutes away from the house. I felt like it was like an epiphany. I felt like I was being led to that Brook I was supposed to drink from that living water. I just knew that this was where I was supposed to attend church.

I went to visit. Now it was Mega Church. It was huge. The parking lot was huge. There were people everywhere. The children had age gaps. So, my oldest daughter would have children's Church in one building, and then my other daughter was a kindergartener. So, she would have Church in another building. And then my son, when he was born, he was an infant, and he would have Church in another building. I would have to get all three of them dropped off and then I could go and sit in the sanctuary and worship. When service was over, I had to pick them all up over again. But I loved every bit of it. I knew this is where I was supposed to be. I knew that there was something drawing me there.

My oldest daughter, she was like it, mom, all of my friends are here. I have so many friends from school and from cheerleading that are here... I like it here. My middle child, as she grew up, she began to have some different experiences there that kind of just drew us even more into that Church and that Ministry. She began to be a part of this youth group that was a part of a Record Label that was a part of her whole entertainment journey. There were so many connections there. Like my husband said, he was hesitant, he was stubborn. He was not wanting to leave his comfort zone. And he stopped attending Church with us.

It made me sad for a bit. I guess I started drawing on my childhood experience. My grandfather and my grandmother not worshiping together. So, I guess I started thinking that it was okay for us to worship in different places. I continued to go there. When it was time for our son to be Christened, I set it all up. I sent the announcements out, and we invited family. My husband had attended some services up to that point but that day, he didn't come. And I thought it was the most selfish thing he could have ever done. Our son was being christened. It's one of the most celebrated times in a Christian's life to have your child dedicated before the Church and dedicated back to the Lord and he wasn't there. I was upset, but we continued and celebrated with the family that did show up and went out and ate dinner afterwards, and I kind of let it go. But in the back of my mind. I just kind of was always a little upset about him not being there for that, but we moved on. Eventually he started coming he started loving it. He started seeing people he knew there, and friends and family and it started to be a staple in our life once again.

To this day we are still members. He eventually joined yes! I joined probably five or six years, before, he joined, and our children joined the Church and that's where we worship today. Now, does he go every Sunday? No. Do I beat him up about it? In the beginning I did, but now I don't. I go, I get the word if I can share something with him I received, I do. If not, he can watch it online. Church has now evolved to streaming online and he can watch online and he kind of prefers to use Sunday as the day he does laundry, he cooks. He's a football fanatic. He'll grow. He'll evolve. I see us worshiping there every Sunday together again as a family. Church is still a big part of who I am and who we are. Our marriage is founded on Godly principles and that's going to remain.

CHAPTER 5

Finances

LEON'S POINT OF VIEW

> *But my God shall supply all your need according to his riches in glory by Christ Jesus. Phil 4:19.*

I never had anyone to teach me financial literacy. In a family that was pretty much extremely poor from my grandmother, working in the fields during the seasons, picking oranges, watermelons, tomatoes and so forth. We grew up just barely getting by. Enough to pay the bills and to put a little food on the table, nothing to splurge and go out and buy name brands, clothes, and shoes, so and so on. As I grew older, I had no one to teach me how to value saving money. No one taught me this in my early years in our marriage there was a time my wife didn't work because we were fairly newlyweds. She had a degree but just didn't get a job so quickly when she moved to Atlanta. I pretty much was the breadwinner. And I remember I would come home on pay day.

I would give her my check and say, hey, put it in the bank, go do what you have to do for us. Taking care of the family meaning, food for the house, clothes for the kids, and paying the bills. And we did that for a couple of years. And I've seen people in my life growing up who did just that. A man would go out and work, bring home the check to mom and she would take care of everything else, the food, bills. I was very clear to my wife that our children would never go without anything. Whatever she felt the kids needed, I want to make sure we provide it. I didn't want our kids growing up the way we grew up or the way I grew up. I grew up having gone without a lot of different things. My wife, she didn't grow up that way. She had a supportive mother and grandparents, and her grandparent was well off and knew about entrepreneurship. That's the difference between us.

However, I was pretty good at saving money even when I was a teenager. I remember my oldest child was being born. I was so excited. I went out and got three jobs that summer. And again, I had this mentality that my child will not want for anything. So, I had three jobs. My grandmother was like, son, when are you going to sleep? But I worked those jobs as long as I could. I mean, I really struggled and struggled to work those three jobs. I worked an overnight job. I would get up early in the morning, work a morning job and get off that job and work an afternoon job before I worked the night job. I was just doing what I thought I had to do to take care of my family. I saved $1000 dollars, probably. But also, I was headed off to school in the fall, and I needed money for school.

I would save every Penny, every dime going off to school. I didn't have anybody going to give me a check or a handful of cash and say, hey, go off, get a great education, and get a better life for yourself. Yeah, I didn't have that. My grandmother couldn't do it. My father certainly couldn't do it. I did what I had to do. I can admit I have blown through a lot of money, just frivolous spending, self-ishness: just didn't put any thought in my spending, knowing I had mouths to feed and responsibilities to take care of. There were times I only thought about me.

My wife and I had a joint bank account. And when she started working her money, and my money would go in that same account. We tried that and for a while it worked. We took care of bills, took care of our children, did what we had to do for finances. But, I was splurging on what I wanted to do. I wanted to go hang out with my friends, buy something to drink, buy name brand shoes and clothes. I didn't worry about tomorrow or the balance of the account. I just did frivolous spending and took no account for anyone else. It was disastrous. Over the years, we had decided that we can no longer share banking account. And, we split the responsibilities of taking care of financial responsibilities that seem to work for us. I would pay what-ever bills that we decided I would pay. She paid whatever bills that we decided she was going to pay and that seemed to work for us. We bought our own cars, put them under my own name. We didn't have the same car insurance. We even had separate cell phone bills. Again, a lot of dumb mistakes. Just wasn't educated on finances. And just like that, a lot of money just went blowing in the wind; just out there, money that we could be saving and investing. Again, no one taught me how to save and invest.

Moving to Atlanta was definitely an eye opener. You see, a lot of wealthy black people doing well and in high position on jobs, such as the Mayor, Police Chiefs, Execu-tives of Fortune 500 companies, and most importantly, a lot of Blacks here in Atlanta owned their own businesses or multiple businesses. I would travel out to the suburbs to my cousin's house and the neighborhood is full of Blacks who own their own homes, not just modest homes. I mean luxury homes 2 to 3 acres. I know it could be done. It was a goal that I wanted to have one day for myself and my family. My own businesses, own my home, maybe several cars. I know that goal was reachable and again, just didn't know how to go about getting it. I felt you get a good education, you get a degree, you're on the job worked 30, 40 years, and you can do all that and more. But I think that's the mentality that my grandparents probably instilled in me at a younger age, so I thought that was the right thing to do to be successful. As I look at it now and back in hindsight you can be an entrepreneur from the beginning. If you have the proper guidance, you have a mentor you can become a successful entrepreneur. Yeah, you can do that straight out the gate. I never had the opportunity to do that.

I dreamed of doing a lot of things after my career, but just didn't work out that way. Well, in too many years in our marriage, I just didn't have that entrepreneurial spirit. On the other hand, my wife, she was gung-ho with it. She wasn't as afraid to try to be the entrepreneur. She tried many things, and I supported her totally.

But sometimes you feel that thing hadn't run this course, and now you don't have a plan B to keep the momentum. I feel that she's gotten better. She's smart. And one thing I know she has going for her, she trusts in the Lord, with all her might, and her faith is strong. She is a Christian. By that I mean she studies the Word of God. By no means am I saying she is perfect. She encourages, uplifts and inspires others to be successful. She often encouraged me to do more and do better. But I seem to always have another agenda. I might not want to hear what she's saying, or I don't want to lose any money. I may not be interested in any ideas of starting my own business. I don't know. I just didn't have that motivation and that drive that she has. And again, she wasn't afraid to try new things. I think that's where we started to have a difference of opinion. She wanted more out of life, more than just going off somebody job, working 40 hours a week for a paycheck.

She wanted more than that. I was stagnant, complacent, didn't feel like rocking the boat. I was working a decent job, making decent wage, decent salary, and I started working a part-time job. Making money on a part-time job. I was making more than probably someone on their full-time job was making it in a whole year. So that was a good opportunity for me. We purchased our first home probably two years after we were married, we built a house from ground up. My second daughter was just born, so she basically was a baby. When we moved into the new home, which was a beautiful time, brand new adventure. With my family, I was ready for the journey, the journey of being a homeowner, just living the life. Even though I had just moved into a brand-new home, I still didn't think about saving money or investing money. My finances pretty much continue to do the same thing. It was just fortunate that I had more money at the time working two jobs, but the lifestyle didn't change much and then another child more responsibilities and just never took it upon myself to save.

We should always have something for that rainy day or have something for the future. Save for your children's College fund. I was young and didn't think about any of those things and again, I wish somebody had taught me about investing my money back then. I could have invested in some of that Apple stock, that somebody could retire by now or something. Finances have never been on my priority list, but it should have been. There were times I didn't agree with my wife and finances. There were sometimes that she has gone behind my back and taken out business loans to start up her business and maybe years ago by I knew nothing about it. I remember this one time she came clean about a loan that she took out for one of her entrepreneurial endeavors. And I don't know, it could have been the guilt that was eating her up or financially paying back the loan could have been a little overwhelming for her. But she told me, and I was a little upset, probably more than a little. But I was definitely not happy about it because being a new homeowner, paying a mortgage and utilities and other necessary financial responsibilities I had to take care of, it felt like we would live check to check. If we wanted to save it didn't seem like we had anything to save because all our money was going toward paying bills, or again we're splurging not thinking about saving any money or investing any money.

She did what she felt was best for our girls. They had to look good. They had to have the best in the way I did too. I think I would have scaled down some expenses for some activities that the girls did. Not saying that would have been the right decision, but at that time I probably would have said something or did something different. But again, my wife wasn't afraid to try.

I hear all the time scared money don't make money. There's a lot of truth into that. Got to spend it to make it. And one thing about my wife, she was not afraid to try. And one thing I love about her, she would definitely put her best foot forward. Anything she do, you're not going to outshine her, you're not smarter, you ain't going to out work her. Over the years as we got older and continued in our marriage, finances became a strain. We couldn't even talk about money and bills. When that came up it would ignite an argument. Finances nearly ruined our marriage, and it's tough to say. Finances is one of the things almost ruined our marriage and it took years for us to come to one accord about finances. I actually had to sit down and listen. I actually had to sit down and be willing to take a risk. And she had some things to learn as well.

There's another saying. They say money is the root of all evil. Well, that could be true. Again, I spoke on this earlier idea, what I wanted to do with my money. I started drinking more, hanging out more, just spending money just because I worked and made it, not thinking of any consequences or any other responsibility that I have, I did what I want to do with my money. Like every Friday for well over ten to twelve years, every Friday I wouldn't even come home from work. On Friday I'll go from work and just hang out at a sports bar, night club or whatever you want to call it. I was in the club because there wasn't a lot of dancing going on, just people hanging around, talking, enjoying my crab legs and good conversation. And I did that for years. The time that I spent at that place, I could have been on another job, working, earning another wage or paycheck. That's where the selfishness came in that I didn't care about what my wife said and how she felt about it. Didn't see my children that day unless I saw them before they went off to school. I felt like I didn't need my wife permission to do what I wanted to do with my time and my money, since I'm the one who's earning it. But that was just bad thinking. When I got married, we became as one. So what's hers is mine and what mines is hers, and we should come together and communicate what we decide to do with our money, with our time. Just bad thinking. And I really wanted some help, probably some good marriage couples I could have reached out to get some correct guidance. But again, I was being selfish, didn't care.

I just wanted to do what made Leon feel good about himself, about whatever good may be going on in his life. I don't know. I felt that's how I celebrated whatever accomplishment that came my way or achieved, and didn't think about my wife and children, how they would feel and what would be my wife's take on it. Finances is something I'm still learning. I like to say I'm getting better at it want to continue to learn better ways to deal with finances and grasp that entrepreneur spirit that my wife so deeply fell in love with. And that'll be one more thing that we will have in common and that we probably could be successful in dealing with. I love the fact that we communicate more. We communicate about everything. We pray about everything. We stand on God's word and have faith that whatever we ask for in his name will come to pass. My life is still teachable moments to this day. I'm learning something regarding finances.

There was a time my wife chose to stay at home and raise our kids and I respected it. I was the breadwinner. I would bring home my paycheck every two weeks and give it to her like clockwork. She would pay the bills, buy groceries, take care of whatever, take care of whatever necessary for us to survive and be able to have enough for extra things. I don't know exactly what she did, but she made it stretch. She would give me $100 for two weeks. Keep in mind, I did very little going out and doing extracurricular activities for those who know me. I didn't drink during this time. I was truly a family man. I wanted to spend all my free time with my wife and my children doing whatever they wanted to do and put a smile on their face.

I saw what I thought were successful people. I saw black men and women owning their own. Black people in high paying profession jobs. I didn't know how they saved or how they worked for their money. I really didn't have anyone to teach me about saving or investing my money and making it work for me in the future. For many years. We live paycheck to paycheck. We live that way due to the lack of financial literacy and probably a lot of stupidity on our parts. Putting our wants before our needs or going about buying the latest shoes or dress. Instead of being responsible and learning how to invest and making money work for you.

There was a time we would give this specific bank nearly $600 in overdraft fees a month. I was not calculating or monitoring the funds in our savings and checking accounts, writing a check and didn't subtract what was in the account. No checks and balances in place. I can be honest and speak in hindsight that I was reckless with our spending and our finances. I wish I had someone to say, Leon, start to do this with your finances. I truly feel we would be better off as a family. There's an old saying in the black community that mothers taught their daughters to save something for a rainy day. Well, my grandmother taught me the same thing. She was the type of person who didn't want me to live off someone else and be irresponsible. Anything I want life I had to go out and earn it, work hard for it and she'll say you appreciate it more if you work hard for it. Over the years that stuck with me and she was absolutely right. Everything I work for, I'm very proud and grateful for everything I have, including my family.

As the years go on, my wife enters the Corporate America. She became the new breadwinner of the family. However, I was still the head of the household. My ego was intact. Manhood was intact. Her professional sales and marketing career allowed her to receive quarterly bonuses and earn trips. She was traveling and the good thing about it our family benefited from it. So, I was not ego tripping that my wife made considerably a lot more money than I did but the money resided in our household, and it benefit our family and we could bless others with our finances as well.

My profession or field is helping others, and it pays less, considerably less money, but I love what I do. I didn't get in my profession for money. I have some very successful people on my father's side of the family retired teacher, retired Air Force men. I look up to these individuals. I highly respect them and if they gave me any type of advice about any parts of my life or what I should do I took that and did my best. I trust anything they told me so I had someone to look up too but I just didn't take advantage as I should have. I wish it was more I want to be in a situation where our finances are so comfortable that we can be able to continue to touch others who are less fortunate. One thing about me is I've always been a giver and my wife even more and what's the use of having finances or money or wealth if you can't share it or bless somebody else. I want to be in a state where I'm financially stable and my family won't have to worry about finances. Neither do or my children. We are blessed abundantly, and we make sure we tithe and give our percentage to our Church. We donate and we make other types of donations to other types of organizations so there's one more than one way you can tithe and give back to the community.

That's something I'm proud of and that my family and my children get to see that we do and I want my children to learn from example so when they're in that situation that they are willing to give back from the heart not that they're supposed to, or they are forced to do something or pressured to do something but genuinely giving from the heart.

CARITA'S POINT OF VIEW

Finances! Okay, how does a newly Wed couple talk about finances or discuss finances or have a plan for finances when it was never discussed in either household? Growing up we knew nothing about what the bills were, how much money came into the house, how much you should save, how much you should invest. We never talked about a budget. We never talked about financial goals. It just was a mute subject in my house. I went to college. I was very adamant about getting my college degree because I knew that would be key to me earning wages and earning an income that would be substantial. I didn't realize that once Leon and I were married and once we started doing this thing called life, how significantly a part finances would play in the marriage. As I began to grow in my career, I earned more money I realized that we should have had a plan.

I remember the first time that I earned a bonus, which at that time was significant to me and our marriage. I earned a $3,000 bonus, and I was like, oh, wow. In addition to my regular pay, it was a bonus. What did we do with the bonus? We took a trip to Vegas, and we parlayed. Once again did not have a structure or a guideline how to handle finances. We had absolutely no clue hindsight 2020, I earned a lot more bonuses and I wish I had saved them. But that's another chapter. But there became a very different dynamic in our household. As my career began to advance, I earned more and more money. And now the head of household became blurred.

Why would I believe that because I earned a significantly amount more money than my husband that I could call the shots? This was a very pivotal point in our marriage. This was a point of a lot of tension and discord. It's the reason most marriages end in divorce. Anyway, as the years began to pass, I began to think more and more that my earnings gave me the right to move into the head of household. When it's very specifically laid out in biblical terms that the man is the head of the house.

I know I did a lot of things for the kids that probably weren't in the best interest... spoiled them. They were spoiled! Leon wanted to pull back and said, hey, that's too much. They don't need all that. They need to earn some things. I wanted to keep giving and giving and giving. I thought giving meant love. Giving meant love, but it was creating less discipline. It was making them weaker. It was not giving them the spirit of wanting to work and work ethic and earning stuff. I was giving them way too much. My mom said it, my husband said it. I didn't get it until they got older and become teenagers and young adults. And I see how this was a detrimental point to the upbringing. But there's always prayer.

Now let's talk about joining finances and joint bank accounts. Listen, that did not work for this marriage. It may work for other marriages. Joint bank accounts did not work for us because in our early years of the marriage, I was paying all the bills, I was doing the budgeting and our monies were joint in the account... men will be men. You know, men like to have money in their pockets. My husband would go to the bank and to the ATM and just withdraw large sums of money. $300 just to have in his pocket as walk around money because he was hanging out with his friends and his buddies. Well, that didn't work because I had already allocated and earmarked that money for bills and for things that were necessities in the house. So, we ended up in situations where our bank account was overdrawn. Overdraft fees, $35, $35... I mean, fees were just hitting our accounts left and right. And the more I would try to have the conversation about this budget. Let's sit down and discuss this. The more bothered he became. We were not on the same page. The more I tried to discuss this with my husband, the more frustrated and irritated and agitated he would be with me because he didn't want to have those conversations.

He felt like his paycheck was there and he could do what he wanted to do. After about five or six years of this, I decided separate bank accounts was how we had to do it. I moved my finances to a different bank and separated it. And that was the most successful thing we could have ever done. He would allocate what he would put toward the bills. I would allocate what I would put towards bills from my account. We would pay those bills and we could save and invest the rest of the money and it worked for us. This is our marriage that worked for us. We hit some of our financial goals and milestones in our life. We bought our first house, our second house.

We could take trips. We could pay for college for our oldest daughter and do things for our younger daughter for her entertainment career and invest in trainers and coaches and all that stuff. We finally could get a grasp and a hold of our finances by separating them. I'm not advocating for this. I'm saying that is what works for us as a married couple. You must find out what works for you. You must decide what is going to be your way of doing things, there is no perfect way, there is our way, and it stopped all the friction concerning money. Money is not the straw that broke the camel's back concerning our marriage. There's another area that really, really, really was the breaking point and we'll discuss that in another chapter.

CHAPTER 6

Head of Household

LEON'S POINT OF VIEW

> Likewise, ye husbands, dwell with them according to knowledge, giving honour unto the wife, as unto the weaker vessel, and as being heirs together of the grace of life, that your prayers be not hindered. 1 Peter 3:7

Head of Household Now I've always figured that out with the head of the household. I'm the man of the house, therefore everyone else should follow my lead, listen to me, obey whatever rules I put in place. That was not the case. I didn't take the head of household role seriously. I didn't see the word of God with being a head of the household. That should have been an honor that I should probably took hold of. But I wanted to play the role of Head of household but didn't want to take on the responsibility that came with it.

I didn't want to lead by example, I ask people to do things you wouldn't do, put rules in places that I don't even follow. So, I think I made it more like a dictatorship instead of a house and a home, loving at home. The role was head of household, and I would throw it in her face. I'm the head of the household and she will be like, prove it. The only thing I can do is to bark profanity and obscenities at her because I felt she was trying to be the head of the household and at the time she was well into her career and she was making excellent money, a good salary, more than me. And I think she felt that since she was making more money, she can play the role of wearing the pants on their family. I know I am not getting to the sexist thing about women wearing dresses or nothing like that, just saying that she played the role of being more at a household and I disagreed with that.

But she could somehow manipulate me into believing that was the way to go. She made the most money, and that had nothing to do with it. Looking back, we thought about this and argued about this for quite some time. And even our children played on this because my wife, they knew she made a considerable amount of money and she wasn't afraid to spend money on the children. Normally if they ask for something, they're going to get it. They want to go somewhere. They're going to go and never have to seek to ask me anything The few times that my daughter or somebody came to ask me anything, I'm on the objective side. Sometimes I'll say no and think about it and change my mind. So, my older daughter got used to me just saying no. Anytime she asked me for anything. So, she stopped asking. She would just go directly to her mom and ask, hey, can I get this or buy me this? Can I go there? Can I hang out with such-and-such, blah, blah, blah? And I will be left in the dark about a lot of things that went on in our home.

Sometimes I felt like my voice wasn't being heard in the house. Another thing that really made me angry and a lot of fights ensued because of it. Police being called to the house, and we would have to go to court. We didn't seek the Bible. We were just doing what we wanted to do but I know I needed to lead by example to show my kids a better way to resolve conflict, teach them how to communicate and think through adversity to be critical thinkers. They didn't often see that in me. Well, I had the capability for doing those things, but I just didn't exhibit them. Especially in front of my children or my wife for that matter. This goes back to when my family and I was visiting two different churches. Now a good man of God and head of household would have never let that happen. But I felt my wife was strong headed.

She went to listen again. She said her soul wasn't being fed at this other Church and she wanted to attend this mega Church and I didn't follow. I couldn't make her stay at the old Church. Not physically I couldn't. She had a made up her mind about what she wanted to do. She did it. I was gung-ho about staying at our original Church. I was involved in the Church. My soul was being fed.

CARITA'S POINT OF VIEW

Ephesians 5:23 makes it clear who should be the head of a household according to God's design for the family: "For the husband is the head of the wife as Christ is the head of the church, his body, of which he is the Savior." A head cannot function on its own. It is as dependent on the rest of the body as the body is on the head.

There are so many things that should be discussed and agreed upon before for a man and a woman enter marriage, and head of household is definitely one of those things. This should be discussed; this should be understood. There should have been a study of the biblical meaning on both parts so that there was a clear understanding of the roles and defining of the roles. We entered this marriage and we kind of fumbled around with this whole head of household thing. It was not clearly defined between Leon and me. We, again, kind of just fumbled in this area.

It is assumed in most Christian households that the man, the male, the husband, should take on the role of head of household. I was okay with him taking on the role of head of household. But then at some point, and I can't place exactly when, but at some point, I began to, I don't know, take it back, if you will. Early in the marriage, I could tell that Leon did not like making decisions, like tough decisions, decisions that we had to say, okay, this has to be handled today, or it could cause the family to go under. It was not good that he just wouldn't decide.

I think it caused him stress. I think that this is my opinion that he didn't like having that burden completely on himself as a head. I like communicating or sitting down and having conversations, not a meeting, but just like coming together and agreeing on what direction we should go. But he didn't really like that approach either. And some things were just time sensitive. I got into a habit of making decisions. I just started deciding without him. The kids would start coming to me and I would just decide. Without discussing it with him. And this went on for years and years and years, and Leon got quiet. Then he shut down on me.

Some days we would get into arguments, and they

would be really big, bad arguments, probably out of frustration and being fed up was the core of some of these arguments. But the line was never clear. It was never understood, it was never discussed, it was never communicated. And we didn't succeed in this area of our marriage. We failed miserably, and it caused us to fail miserably in other areas of our marriage. After reading and getting a better biblical understanding of it, it's not a dictatorship. It's not that the head of household gets to dictate what the wife does, and she has to be a puppet. And that whole "S" word, that submissive word is also feared by the woman. If I submit, am I weak? If I submit, do I lose my identity? What is that all about?

These are all things we should have been discussed, understood and defined prior to entering marriage. I think marriage is so much more than picking out a wedding gown and sending invitations or gathering your friends and relatives to be bridesmaids and groomsmen and the color of the bridesmaid dresses and the venue and the food and the photographer and videographer. That is not marriage. The money should be poured into, I believe, marriage counseling, marriage Ministry, investing in marriage courses, going to perhaps even a marriage retreat prior to getting married.

It's just there's so many things that need to be understood and need to be taught in so many areas that should have been communicated prior to… and this head of household has to be settled. It must be decided. So, for years I made all the decisions, and it was weighty. It was heavy. It was very burdensome. I wanted him to help me decide, but he became very elusive and very non committed to making decisions and very no, you've done it like this for so long. So, you continue in your way and take the fall and take the failure in your decision or take the glory in it. It caused me a lot of stress. I began to gain a lot of weight because eating was my outlet. I didn't drink alcohol. I didn't do drugs. I didn't hang out. I started medicating my stress and fear and heartache from this whole head of household thing with food, which is never good. You know, everything we do in life should be done in moderation.

I found out that we had to come together. We had to show a United front, especially in front of the children. We're going to talk about discipline in another chapter. But had we shown a United front early in our marriage, we would have alleviated so many pitfalls, so many arguments, so many stressful moments, so much tension. Had we just had the understanding and communication of head of household, it would have fixed a lot of things that kind of went awry in the marriage. We figured it out on child number three, probably by the time he was about ten years old. He's 16 now, but that's about when we figured it out. Our son was ten our second child was 15 and oldest child was 21. When we got it, all figured out, yeah, it was a little late and some of the damage had been done. And we own that. The head of household is responsible for that. As a couple, as parents, as married partners, we own not having a handle on it.

We have it now!! We can show an example for our grandchildren and great grandchildren. We can show that love, is first, it should be the underlying tone and foundation of it all. Love should be the foundation. When love is the foundation, then everything else can build on top of love. Communicate with sweet lips and understanding. Go in trying to understand the other person's point of view from a place of love and not a place of wanting to be right and prove yourself right. With all these walls and barriers that we put up. No let's operate in love, let's communicate in love, let's coexist in love. Love should be the premise of it all. We got that now. We can always show affection in front of the children. We show affection while we're out. We just we got the love thing down and respect is the other thing. Respect, respect, respect your spouse. Respect them, don't correct them, or judge them in public. Have conversations that are private in private.

We figured it out. We got it and I don't want to say it's too late. I don't ever want to say it's too late, but we got it now. We figured it out. We have a firm understanding of it and life is good! Marriage is good! We can do an eternity now because we got it.

CHAPTER 7

Discipline

LEON'S POINT OF VIEW

I was raised different from this younger generation. As I stated before, I didn't grow up in a two-parent home. I was raised by my grandmother, who exhibited much love and little discipline. She was a small, petite woman who really couldn't whip her grandchildren as she would like to. We were at an age where we didn't get whippings. Maybe the school called she would cuss us out, but no punishment. I didn't have devices she would take away to punish me. Like back then there was Atari, and hand video games, she couldn't take any of that away. It wasn't a form of discipline, but I remember one time I was talking back. I actually talked back to my grandmother, and she took a broom, and I turned away, not knowing anything. She threw it and hit me in the back of my leg and broke the broom. I never talked back since that day. But of course, we can't do that now because that would be considered child abuse and cruel, and you can go to jail.

I tried to be the disciplinary person in my family. My kids would always gravitate to their mom more like she was the good cop, and I was the bad cop. Of course, I was a bad cop. She was a good cop. And sometimes they'll come ask me for certain things, and my immediate answer would be no. But that's who I was. I just say no, and then I go to her and then she'll make the decision, okay, yeah, you can go here, or you can get this and so forth. Many times, that I was not brought into discussion when it concerned the kids. She would make many decisions but did not involve me. That was an issue for me that probably created a bunch of arguments and fights in our marriage, kids playing us against each other. That was a bigger problem. Now it was hard for me. Well, take that back. It was not hard for me to chastise my children. I didn't have a problem not sparing the Rod. Occasionally I did. But again, it is brought more strife into our marriage. My wife felt I would discipline my children out of anger. Sometimes she was right. I didn't realize I was doing that.

CARITA'S POINT OF VIEW

Growing up discipline for me was also a part of loving us. I knew that when my mother disciplined us, it was because she loved us. You see, growing up in a household with other siblings, I have an older brother (he did not live in the house with us) and two sisters. My mother was a single mother, and our grandparents lived in close proximity. They lived maybe a mile and a half away, less than a five-minute drive. So, if you were disciplined at home with my mother, you best believe that you were going to be disciplined a second time once we got to our grandparents' house. They had the village mentality, so we kind of walked a very straight and narrow path. At least my twin sister and I did, because we knew that discipline meant that you would get it twice home and at grandparents' house. I always wanted to discipline my children with love.

I didn't mind my husband disciplining the children, but I quickly found out that he didn't understand how to discipline with love. It was very hard for me to watch and tolerate my husband take his frustrations out on the children. If he was aggravated by something that happened between, he and I or something that happened at work, he would come home and take it out on the kids. That wasn't fair, so I would always intercede and jump in. I probably should have pulled him aside in private during those moments, but I was like Mama Bear, and I would jump to their defense because I knew exactly what he was doing, I don't believe that when you discipline a child that you should call them out of their name. I don't believe that children should be called curse words and I don't believe you should lower a child's self-esteem while disciplining them.

It should be the opposite. If you take the time to discipline them with love, it will raise their self-esteem versus disciplining out of anger and frustration and calling them names, it lowers their self-esteem, makes the children angry and bitter children and then here we go with a vicious, ugly cycle. I had to intercede. I had to step in. I could not allow Leon to do this to them, and I know he was only operating out of experience. I know he was doing what he thought was right, and I had no doubt in my mind that he loved them. But I knew how detrimental it could be to discipline in that manner. So, yes, I take full responsibility for the strife created in our marriage around discipline. Many times, I should have pulled my husband to the side after and talked to him about what I observed and the way that I felt he was handling the kids. But it just would hit me with such a rage, and I had such a wanting to protect them I would do it in front of the children. And then, of course, that showed that Leon and I were not on the same page. It created even more problems for the children and for the marriage, because that didn't serve anybody, that didn't serve our family at all.

And once the kids became older, they thought it was okay for them to talk back to my husband and disrespect my husband. It made them assume the rules could be broken as soon as he left their presence. It caused a lot of heartache. Discipline was a very, very touchy subject for our family, and I believe it hurt my oldest child the most, because by the time Leon and I were married, my oldest daughter was five years old. So, she was old enough to see and hear and understand everything that was going on. Hearing the arguments about discipline, us, trying to figure out how to be parents. It wasn't like we did it while she was a baby and then figured out what to do when she really couldn't hear or understand. But she was old enough that she knew what was going on. She could hear the arguments, and it really hurt her a lot.

Although I know she's forgiven us for a lot of it, I still believe that there's more healing that needs to happen, and I'm prayerful about it. That is one reason we are writing this book. We don't want other young couples to have to deal with the things that we dealt with. We're hoping this book in some way, shape or form will be a guide or roadmap, at least so they'll know the things to avoid. They can avoid some pitfalls that we fell into, some traps that we fell into. They can have good dialogue before they get to the point of no return.

JUST DANCE WITH ME 59

At some point in the marriage, probably after 15 years, Leon and I understood we must present a United front in the presence of the children. Regardless of how we felt about one another, or the other parent's way of doing discipline, we would not speak about it in front of the children. We would not communicate discord in front of the children. As far as they were concerned, we were on the same page. One band, one sound, and if one said no, the other said no. If we needed to discuss something, then we would call the other parent into the room. If it was over the phone, we would get the other parent involved. That way, the children couldn't play us against each other. That way, Leon and I had a chance to discuss and come up with our plan of action. And the children no longer thought they could get away with things. They no longer tried to play one parent against the other. And it created a more loving environment. It created a better household, and my son gets to benefit the most from that because he's the only minor that's still at home with both parents. My daughters are both adults and have moved out. But they see the United front now and when they come around, the atmosphere is so much more pleasant.

We figured it out. You are supposed to as the saying goes, correct him in private and compliment him in public. Yeah, we got it figured out now and our prayer is that other couples learn how to pivot and just dance through discipline.

CHAPTER 8

Separation

LEON'S POINT OF VIEW

> And unto the married I command, yet not I, but the
> Lord, Let not the wife depart from her husband: But and
> if she depart, let her remain unmarried or be reconciled
> to her husband: 1 Corinthians 7:10-11

Separation. This is probably one of the worst chapters in this book for me and I hated being away from my family. As I mentioned before, I was an angry person due to my past circumstances. I didn't have my parents. My mom died when I was a baby. My father wasn't always there. I wasn't born with wealth; I wasn't loved as a child. All these things contributed to all the anger I had built up inside me. There came a time when I had to release that anger. Unfortunately, the target for my anger was my wife and kids. I was abusive in so many ways until my wife was fed up with me. The first time I recall separation came when me and my wife disagreed on how I chastise my children, keep in mind my kids play on their parents all the time. They play their parents against each other.

I was known as the bad cop parent, and she was known as the good cop parent. My wife and I will begin to argue objects are thrown and quickly the argument becomes physical. My wife gives so much, and I can't deal with that. The children are scared and crying, and she calls the police. They show up, assesses the situation, separate us, and asking a lot of probing questions. Neither my wife nor I have any marks bruises on our bodies so no one will go to jail. But she elects to leave the home with the kids, and I wasn't having it. But due to my disagreement led to me to use profanity in front of the children, which led me going to jail that night.

I'll take that back. Our first separation was in East Point, Georgia. We were married less than a year. My wife and I started to argue because I wanted to go out and hang with my fraternity brothers at a function and she wanted me to stay at home. Of course, I disagreed with her, and I was attempting to leave she took my keys and hid them from me. Prior to that, we had gotten into a physical altercation with each other and at that time there were scratches and bruises on both of us. I thought I was doing the right thing to defuse the situation by walking to the church's chicken where there was a pay phone, and I was going to call the police to make her give me my keys. To make a long story short, the police came, and we both went to jail. I had to call my cousin to take custody of our child. To make matter worse, my wife and I spent the New Year in jail. I felt so freaking horrible about how I handled the situation and how I let my family down. I brought my family and neighbors into my personal life. This whole situation was an unfortunate event and was humiliating.

Over the years we continue to be together but often

separated. When it came to our children and financial affairs and many other responsibilities, we both shared. I can recall another very unfortunate time we were separated. My wife was very slick with this separation. She was strategic and very well planned out to get me out of the house. Planning probably took some time and well thought out just came from a couple of weeks not talking or sleeping in the same bed together. thought we were hurting each other by not talking to each other. Well, in my case, it did hurt me. My wife suddenly talked to me on this early Saturday morning.

She was out running errands as she wouldn't normally do. She called me while I was leaving the barbershop and I informed her I was on my way home. She said, okay, I'll meet you at the home prior to me hanging up the phone. As I arrived in our cul-de-sac, there were two Clayton County Sheriff cars parked in front of my neighbor's house. Of course, I'm thinking there must be an issue at their home. So, I continue to drive into my garage, and I can see the sheriff cars are in my driveway. Now my suspicion grows to immediate concern. What the hell are you doing at my house? I'm saying to myself. One officer asked if I was Leon Montgomery. I replied, yes. He responded by saying, I'm here to serve you with this PTO temporary Protection order on behalf of your spouse, Carita Montgomery. I was ordered to pack all my clothes that I can and leave the home. Believe me, I was taken by surprise with her well thought out plan. So, I was escorted from my home with several onlooking neighbors as I exit the house with several bags in my hand and strapped on my back. I'm going through so many emotions hurt, betrayed, and embarrassed, just to name a few. The officer took the keys to my home, my garage opener, and I was informed to refrain from making any contact with my wife and children. Man, I tell you, this is one of the worst feelings I have ever had. Probably the first time I felt alone and abandoned. The family I knew for so many years I knew no more. I had no idea where I was going to lay my head down for the night. So of course, I call relatives and close friends for a place to stay. I end up going to stay with my very close cousin in Austell, Georgia. His wife was very understanding to what I was going through, and they both agreed to allow me to stay in their basement as long as I need it.

I was so angry and bitter about what had happened to me. My cousin and I talked about what transpired up to this point. He gave me some of the best advice I've ever received in my life, but I felt it was just a little too late. He said just let it play out and see what will become of this unfortunate situation. That night, I laid my head down in a strange but comfortable environment. Comfortable meaning that I was still around some close family. I thought of all the different ways I could have done things different. My mind was racing with so many scenarios. I recall what led up to this separation. It was a discipline issue with my oldest child.

I didn't think it through when trying to deal with an inappropriate display of behavior with my daughter. I let my anger lead me into a bad direction where I became physical with her. Of course, I regret all my actions. My wife and I have different discipline styles and backgrounds with discipline over our own children. I stayed with my cousin for nearly a month.

There was a court hearing also in place. I went to court, and the judge allowed us to talk with a mediator prior to the actual hearing. So we talked, and I learned she didn't want to continue to be separated or divorce was not on the table at this time and divorce was not on the table. At the hearing, I agreed to everything was my fault, and I was willing to do what it takes to be with my family again. We both wanted the same thing. To be honest, I truly disobeyed that TPO. I constantly called and text my wife and I didn't care about going to jail. My family was my number one and I would do what it takes to get them back. The Lord put this family together, and he trusted me to keep it together. My Lord, I didn't want to let him down.

I wish I could tell you that was my last separation, but I would be lying. The common thread has always been discipline. It comes to our children. But there is a certain behavior you don't expect your children to exhibit towards your parents. So, my wife played from her same playbook and got me removed from the home again. I was removed from my home again.

During my departure from my home. My wife had a different plot. Within a couple of weeks away from each other. She asked me to lunch. She met with me and wanted to inform me our children that we will be permanently moving to another place. She and the kids would be permanently moving to another place until further notice or until we're able to work out our differences. I immediately raised up from the table and refused to honor her with that request because she made this decision without me. I never want her to uproot my kids and move away I would not go along with this because it would help ease her guilt for uprooting the kids from their home and their father.

My wife went on to rent an apartment in Fayetteville, Georgia. However, my children were still attending school in Clayton County, and I was seeing my kids daily. We were separated for a year. I was living in my big house alone with my dog Holliwood. I started to visit my kids in Fayetteville even more over time Carita and I talked more and eventually mended our relationship. I moved to Fayetteville and rented out my house. Also doing this separation I moved from my cousin's house in Austell, Georgia and I moved closer to my family with a friend that I've been known for nearly 20 years and once again I moved into a basement.

This time this basement was not in the best condition and deplorable I was living with dogs in cages with bad older I didn't really have much worse condition. I had to do what I had to do. It's just a very uncomfortable situation at the time but thank God it was short lived. I only stayed there a couple of weeks and I was back with my family once again I wouldn't put my worst enemy through what I experienced. Let me just give some details. My friend and wife didn't want me to stay there which I understand her reasons. One reason was she had a young teenage daughter in the home. Somehow, I could stay there for a couple of weeks. I'm back in the basement and I hated. I was grateful and dealt with another unfortunate situation. I was just so happy to be close to my family. I wasn't back home but close enough to touch them. I found myself going driving by the house just to take a glimpse of them in the yard or in the driveway. Plane.

CARITA'S POINT OF VIEW

What bride goes into a marriage thinking that there's a possibility for separation. I didn't think that thought that I was going to be in the honeymoon stage forever. Well, unfortunately, that's just not the way it is unless you are prepared mentally and physically well equipped, knowing how to communicate with your spouse, knowing how to handle conflict, if these things have not been instilled in you oh, by the way, lots and lots of prayer. But if these things have not been instilled with you or in you, then separation is inevitable.

Most of the separations in this marriage were initiated by me. Yes. This is how I dealt with the tension, the conflict, the arguments, the fighting, the fighting that really got out of hand. I dealt with it by separating either myself from Leon, my husband, or having him separated and taken away from the home just so that things could settle back down around me. Is this right? No, but it was the only way that I knew how to deal with it. The very first separation I remember is 1999.

We had been married for one year. The fighting was just bad, and it was getting to where Leon had become physical, meaning he was fighting me with his hands and his fists. And I remember thinking, there's just no way that this is what God meant for me. I had money that came in from a car accident. I was rear-ended in Atlanta on one of the interstates, and the money, it was a small amount, maybe like $2,000 had finally hit my account and the fighting began and I literally grabbed my daughter Nia, who was the only child we had went to the Atlanta airport, purchased a ticket for the next flight, leaving for Sarasota. I wasn't working a full-time job. I was a temp staff worker, and she was out for the summer. This was around end of July going into the first week of August or so, and school hadn't started back.

And I literally packed up what I could go to my mom's

house, and I was there for like two weeks and didn't take any of Leon's phone calls. My mother didn't disclose where I was. He called and called her house over and over. And I didn't have a cell phone. And that was our first separation. I eventually came back, and we eventually worked it out. And then shortly thereafter, I became pregnant with our second child, my second daughter. But it was rough. It was very rough, but I understood the power of prayer and I just continued to just pray through it.

The second separation, 2004, I think that's right. But again, Leon just started drinking a little more, and he became more and more angry and unruly and had this very petty, tit for tat mentality and just wasn't good to live with. It was just unbearable. And I remember this one day we had this huge argument, and I went down to the police station, and I filed the very first temporary protective order, one of several that would be filed throughout this 23-year marriage. But I filed it, and they served it. He was put out of the house for 30 days. And I remember that being close to like Memorial Day. It was a holiday, something around there. And I was going home to Florida anyway for the holiday to be with family. And I was getting ready to drive home. He didn't want me to go or for whatever reason. And he became angry and physical and all of that.

The next temporary protective order that I can remember was 2013. It should have been a time of great joy, great excitement in our family. My son was born at this time. He was like seven or eight years old. My daughter, the second child, the middle child, she had gotten the greatest opportunity to go on to X Factor out in Los Angeles, California. And right before we left to go again. I don't know if something angry, some jealousy, some envy or whatever that sparked. And my husband, he did not know how to express himself and did not know how to talk about what he was frustrated about. And he just took it out on everybody in the house. It just was, again, unpleasant to be around him. Now, don't get me wrong. When he was good, he was good. He was the funniest, loving, kind gentleman that you want to be around. He was poetic. He was spontaneous. He was always buying me gifts all throughout the marriage. Leon always bought gifts. That's his love language to give gifts. I'm not a very materialistic person, so I really didn't need the gifts. I would rather you be the loving, kind husband without all the anger and the arguing rather than the gifts. I didn't get into all the jewelry and designer this designer that it just wasn't me. But he showered me with gifts, nonetheless.

What happened in 2014 is probably the most hurt I felt in the entire marriage. It was New Year's Eve, leading into 2015 and my husband was in another one of his angry seasons, if you will. And he got into an argument with my daughter's manager at the time in the entertainment industry. I don't know why he was so angry because our life was good. At least I thought it was. After the argument he went on Facebook and did a rant. The same group that had gotten my daughter, to the X Factor was the same group that the manager put my daughter out of because of my husband. She also missed the opportunity to go to the Grammy Awards because of his actions. And it literally ate me up on the inside. I could not get over it. I could not let it go. I could not stop reliving the moment. I hated him in the worst way. I sometimes get teary eyed to this day when I think about it, because my daughter had worked so hard, and she earned it. She earned the right to go to the

Grammy Awards. And it was snatched away from her because of what he had done. I was not just upset with him, but I really was like, done. We stopped having sex. I stopped even wanting him sleeping in the same room. This went on for 5 months. And of course, the longer it went on, the more frustrated and angrier and physical he wanted to get.

I remember the very day that I filled out an application for an apartment. I was approved on the spot. I got the apartment. I went to rooms to go, and I got approved for furniture. The kid's bedroom was furnished.

My daughter, the oldest was in college, so I didn't really have to worry about a place for her. But the other two, 2nd daughter was 14 and my son was 9. I made sure that they had at least a bed and bedroom furniture. I didn't have a bed. I got an apartment, and I didn't live in it at first. Fear set in. I had it for over 30 days, maybe 45 days before I lived in it. Mother's Day weekend 2015, he had one of his big explosive rants, and that was it. The police were called. They didn't arrest him but asked him to leave for the night. I bagged up everything that I could bag up for the kids and me. I threw it in my car, and I left and got into the apartment. This time, he knew I was done. He started going to Church and reading his Bible. He started just telling me how much he really wanted our marriage to work, sending me letters and meeting us at Church on Sunday and just really, really wanting to mend and bring the marriage back together. But we stayed separated for almost a year. Then finally I let him come back to the apartment, and we put a renter in the house.

In 2016 we were blessed to buy our second home. We moved into the home, my husband lost his job and the fighting and arguing all started all over again. It was like an

awful nightmare. And in 2017 I had to do a third temporary protective order against my husband. And the crazy
thing is, when the Hurricane, I want to say it was Irma
came through Atlanta. He was out of the house. He was
living in his car at this time, he was too embarrassed to call
friends because he knew he had kind of burnt all those
bridges. They were like, no, you need to start looking in the
mirror. So, he was literally living out of his car. My daughter, my middle child, the forgiving one, the loving one, my
mini me, she was like, mom, just give him one more chance.
Let them come back. And I did.

In 2018, a lot of my husband's drinking caught up with
him, and he had gotten a DUI, which was his second DUI.
And this time, the separation wasn't nothing that I initiated.
It was something that he caused. And he had to do three
months in jail. This was probably the most pivotal turning
point of our marriage, because when he came out, I saw for
the first time that all the anger wasn't out of being mean, a
big, bad Wolf. It was out of fear. For the first time, I saw
fear in my husband's eye when he thought he could go
back. My outlook on our marriage and on communication
with him completely changed. I've never called the police
since. I've never raised my voice to the point of us having
physical altercations again. I knew I was dealing with a
person who had so much fear in him, that fear caused him
to be angry.

I decided I had to love on this man. I had to love on
him. He grew up without a mother. He grew up without his
father being in his life. He grew up with a grandmother
where it was a hostile situation. He just never, ever had love,
someone to love him unconditionally. And I knew it was
time for us to operate in love. No more arguments.

CHAPTER 9

Pandemic

LEON'S POINT OF VIEW

> *The glory of this latter house shall be greater than of the former, saith the LORD of hosts: and in this place will I give peace, saith the LORD of hosts. Haggai 2:9.*

I don't think there was a time we have been closer or spent so much time together. We spent weeks to months together talking and doing new things. No one in my family ever would have thought we would be living through a pandemic. Our nation was hit hard with a devastating virus called Coronavirus Disease 2019 (COVID-19) and people was suddenly dying. This pandemic scared me to where I was afraid to leave my home. I was afraid for my children. I wanted them to be safe from COVID-19. Local businesses and restaurants started to close. My favorite bar closed, and I had nowhere to go for a beer and good conversation. This pandemic hit the work force, and I was thrust into working from home. It was a relief but a little scary working from home. I literally had to work solely through emails and Zoom conferences. It was at this point I learned that a lot of jobs can be performed from home. Working from home brought me a lot of freedom. I can honestly say abused a lot of the freedom I had working from home. I started to binge watch television shows, walked my dog, and perform chores around the house while working from home. My wife didn't have the luxury of working from home. I guess her Corporate America wasn't having it. Anyhow, I got used to being at home and started to spend more time in our back yard. My wife would come home from a long hard day at work to dinner and a party in the backyard. This was the birth of The Backyard Party. My wife hated I was home and having so much fun. I wasn't stressed. I did less complaining. I was open to doing different things. I had the party started by the time she got home. It didn't take my wife long to fall into party mode. We started rolling the speaker out the backyard. We had wine and beer on deck. We ate seafood every weekend for well over a year. And we just dance. We had a great time enjoying each other's company. We danced to old tunes, and we slow dragged.

I consider the pandemic a curse and a blessing. Unfortunately, the pandemic took so many untimely lives. No one knew what to expect from the pandemic. People did what they can to stay safe from COVID-19. But on the other hand, the pandemic brought me closer to my wife and family. My wife and I talked more about everything. Carita and I would hangout more and take daily dates together. We would cuddle together on the coach or schedule time for a business meeting.

I didn't realize how much I was taken my wife for granted. Prior to the pandemic, I selfishly went about my way and didn't consider my wife feelings at all. This pandemic allowed me to realize how much I appreciate and value her. She has always encouraged me to be my best and strive for pure excellence in all that I do. She constantly prays for me and our entire family daily. I didn't realize how much I was missing when it came to my wife. I enjoy dancing with her though this pandemic. I can say a lot of positive things have come out of this pandemic. We are closer now. We are as one with our children and decision making as it affects this family. The pandemic also births a few opportunities for me and my wife. We thought of co-writing this book during the pandemic.

However, my wife is a talker. She loves to discuss ways to make money and be prosperous. There are countless times I didn't want to hear that because I had my own agenda. I just wanted to be left alone and do what I wanted to do. The pandemic opened my eyes and made me realized she was merely trying to share something she is so passionate about with me. She constantly listens to me when I talk about football, players and stats. She entertained me because just because. Marriage is built on more than love; it's built on understanding your spouse and giving them what they need at that time. The pandemic taught me that every word, thought, and emotion must be reciprocated. The pandemic showed me how to love better, give more and appreciate all I have been blessed with. The pandemic saved me, my marriage and family.

CARITA'S POINT OF VIEW

Every Friday was a special day. We couldn't wait to get in our backyard and just dance. This was March, April, May, June, July, and August. And throughout the holidays, every

Friday was like celebration day. We danced all our problems away. We danced all our issues away. At the end of 2020 we took a trip to Las Vegas because I was going to be turning 50 years old at the top of 2021. We danced, and we laughed, and we enjoyed each other so much. In, 2021, we vowed to just do as much together as we possibly could, and we traveled, and we danced, and we laughed, and we traveled a lot more and we enjoyed each other. We fell in love again. The pandemic healed our marriage.

2020, the pandemic hits, and we're all stuck at home; well, he was home, and the children were home. And I had a job as a management executive, so I had to go in. Oh, he couldn't go out drinking. He couldn't go to the sports bars anymore. And we were just home. This is where just dance really hit me. Every Friday, we would go, and we would get a big seafood feast, crab legs and shrimp and boiled eggs, sausage, and all that. And we would go out on the back patio, and we would just dance. We called it the "Backyard Party". How many of you know that this was not at all about the party? It was more about two people who finally after 22 years of marriage could see each other. Finally, all the layers of life were peeled back, and we could love each other for who we are and not what society wanted us to portray. When the world stopped, we had no more outside demands on our time other than work so we could focus on each other. My husband asked in a previous chapter why I stayed? I just had faith that I would one day have everything, and now I do. We titled this book "Just Dance with Me" because dance is a universal language. Dance requires both persons to move in sync and to rhythm and beat, in harmony. When couples dance someone takes the lead and the other follows. When a man and woman are in sync, she can naturally allow him to lead, but he also allows her to display her dance moves naturally and gracefully without overshadowing or impeding upon them. Marriage is a series of dances. Sometimes you close your eyes, sometimes you look your partner directly in the eye and other times you get a glimpse of the crowd watching you move.

I wish we could have led our marriage with this concept of dancing but that was not our journey. We are also not advocating sticking around in situations that are toxic, abusive, unsafe and life threatening. We love the institution of marriage and feel like our mistakes and misfortune can help someone else avoid them all together. Also don't be afraid to reach out for help. There is nothing good about being on an island by yourself in isolation. We love the concept of marriage support groups, marriage ministries, couple nights, marriage vent sessions (something we did with other couples in the early years) all of the above. Also don't be afraid to go to marriage counseling both spiritual and clinical. I say fight for your marriage if it is worth fighting for. But by all means if it has to be dissolved then do so with no guilt or condemnation. Whether you stay or go it is your decision to make and no one can make you feel one way or another about it.

This chapter and this book are about healing, growing, prevention, patience and more for other marriages not our own. We have been totally transparent over the last 9 chapters to help couples navigate through the difficulties of marriage. I believe many marriages can be saved, or we can prevent couples from entering something they are not ready for if we are honest and truthful up front. Let's stop painting the fairytale but give real life tools, lessons, support, and information that newlywed and young couples can use. We didn't touch on sex and intimacy in our marriage which is also very important. That is one area that we got right from the start. Having good sex will help you weather the storms. You should always seek to physically please your spouse or partner and Leon has always taken great care of my needs and I have reciprocated. The pandemic probably amplified our sex life, heck what else was there to do (smile).

CHAPTER 10

Just Dance with me

LEON'S POINT OF VIEW

There are always outsiders fighting for against your marriage. Not all people in your corner are fighting for your success. Just dance with me is acknowledgement of flaws, differences of opinions, and respect. Just dance with me assists with hurt, pain and ways to heal. Just dance with me calms the troubled waters, overcome life plights, and endure adversity. Just dance with me gives strength, courage to fight and the spirit of forgiveness. Just dance with me is our way of life. No matter what life throws at us, we are going to dance. We are going to dance to our own tune and our own beat. Meaning Leon and Carita are making the music. We going to dance to the songs that work for this marriage. Just dance with me is your truth and you must live it with your spouse to the full extent. Your marriage is like many types of genres of music, Christian, hip hop, jazz, pop & R&B/Soul. Your marriage will encounter genres of problems like family, finances, infidelity, and illness. I honestly have to say that God plays a major role in what type of genre of music you both will dance to. God is going supply that medium between your different genre of music. I love all types of music!!! Carita loves gospel, pop, and some hip hop. But we are going to dance regardless of the genre of music. Since the pandemic, we just dance through whatever challenges come our way. I speak for my wife, it's not always easy but through faith love will conquer all. I truly pray our dance journey will help other marriages reach its full potential. I bow to you. Owt...

CARITA'S POINT OF VIEW

What he said!! Leon and Carita signing off – We Owt...

www.ingramcontent.com/pod-product-compliance
Lightning Source LLC
Chambersburg PA
CBHW032153020426
42334CB00016B/1268